Fire

Words by Edward E. Daub

Professor
General Engineering Department
University of Wisconsin—Madison

Raintree Childrens Books

Milwaukee

Cover Photo: Larry Shapiro

Library of Congress Number: 87-20799

2 3 4 5 6 7 8 9 0   92 91 89 88

Printed and bound in the United States of America

Library of Congress Cataloging in Publication Data

Daub, Edward E.
  Fire.

  Bibliography: p. 48
  Summary: Discusses fire, its usefulness to man, and
its destructive elements.
    1. Fire—Juvenile literature. [1. Fire] I. Title.
QD516.D27   1987   541.3′61   87-20799
ISBN 0-8172-3254-0 (lib. bdg.)
ISBN 0-8172-3279-6 (softcover)

Fire

Fire helps us control our world. Fire lets us heat our homes and cook our food. Fire gives us light so we can see when it is dark.

    Fire can also be our enemy. A fire can get out of control. Then it moves quickly, destroying almost everything in its path. Every year fire does great harm to buildings, fields, and forests. Fires kill and injure many people and animals.

The first people lived without fire. They were cold at night and in the winter. They ate their food raw because they could not cook it.

They knew that fire was dangerous. They had seen lightning start fires that destroyed trees and animals.

We don't know when people first
controlled fire. Some time long ago, people
bravely took burning branches from trees
that had been hit by lightning. They
learned to use fire. They learned to cook
their food. Fire kept them warm and drove
dangerous animals away.

People later learned ways to start their own fires. One way was to rub two pieces of wood together rapidly. The rubbing made the wood get hot and start to glow. People would blow on the glowing wood to make a flame.

Another way to make fire was to twist a hollow stick while pressing it against a hole in wood. The wood around the hole became hot and began to glow. The person could blow through the stick while twisting it.

Later, people found easier ways to make fire. They hit a piece of steel against a flint to make a spark. The spark set fire to pieces of dried cloth or bark called tinder.

Today we have matches to start a fire. We strike them against a rough strip on the side of the match box. They burst into flame.

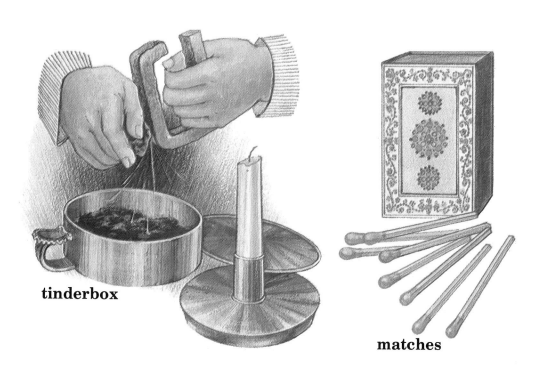

tinderbox

matches

Things that we
burn to make heat or
power are called fuels.
Fuels need oxygen in
order to burn. One-
fifth of the air
is oxygen.

Candles can burn
in open air. But if
a jar is put over
the candle, it will
go out. That is
because the flame
uses up all the
oxygen in the jar.

If a fuel is
burned in a small,
closed space, it can
make an explosion.
Fuels give off gas
when they burn. If
a fuel burns very

fast, it gives off
a lot of gas. The
gas cannot fit in the
small space, so it
bursts out. That is an
explosion.

Some kinds of
burning are very slow.
When iron rusts, it is
really burning in
oxygen. This burning
happens so slowly that
you can't feel the heat.

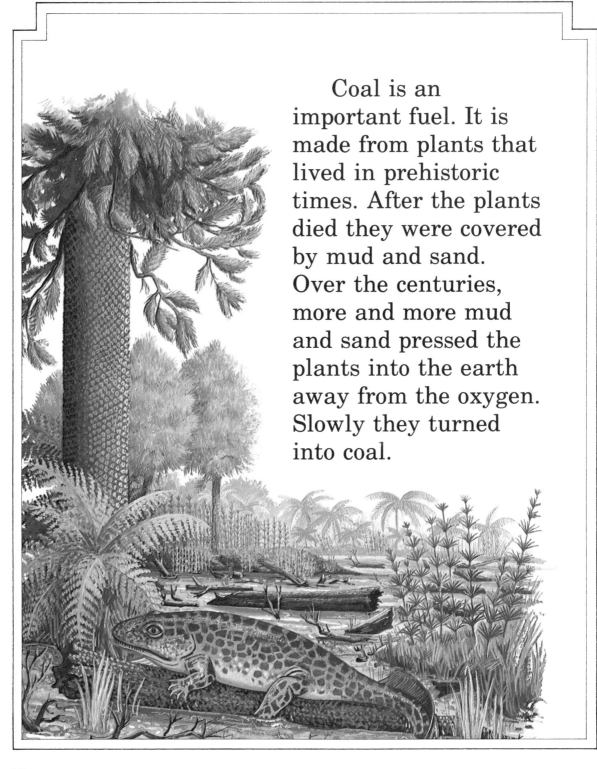

Coal is an important fuel. It is made from plants that lived in prehistoric times. After the plants died they were covered by mud and sand. Over the centuries, more and more mud and sand pressed the plants into the earth away from the oxygen. Slowly they turned into coal.

Most coal is deep underground. Miners dig holes to find a "seam" of coal. Then they dig tunnels along the seam. Miners remove the coal from the ground. Electric cars carry the coal through the mine. Elevators take it to the surface.

Some coal is near the surface of the ground. Removing the coal is called strip mining. When the coal is gone, the land is repaired so that people can use it again.

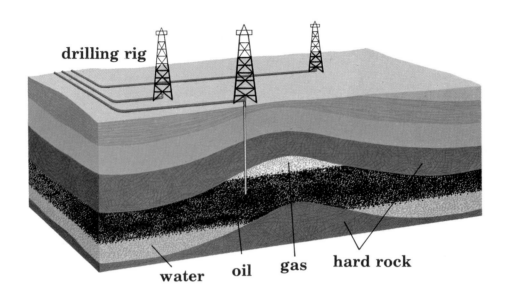

drilling rig

water   oil   gas   hard rock

Oil is another important fuel. Like coal, it is found under the ground. It is made from plants and tiny animals that died and decomposed millions of years ago.

Pipes are sent deep into the earth to reach the oil. It is found between layers of hard rock. Oil is made into gasoline for cars, fuel for jet airplanes, and heating oil for furnaces.

drilling platform

Natural gas is another fuel that people often use. It is also found under the ground, usually with oil. Sometimes oil and gas are found under the floor of the sea. If the sea is deep, drilling platforms are built on the water above the fuel site. Pipes carry the fuel to the land.

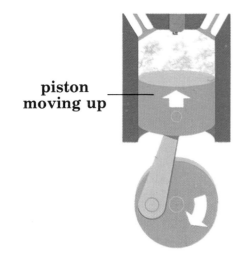

piston moving up

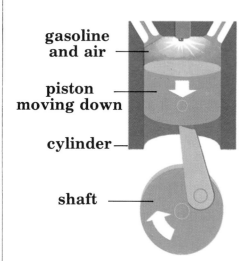

gasoline and air

piston moving down

cylinder

shaft

We burn fuels to run our machines. Gasoline and air are mixed in the carburetor to run car engines. A piston in the engine cylinder first draws the mixture into the cylinder and then squeezes it into a small space. Then an electric spark lights the gasoline and air. The mixture explodes, and the hot gases push the piston down. The piston turns a shaft, which makes the wheels go around.

JET ENGINE

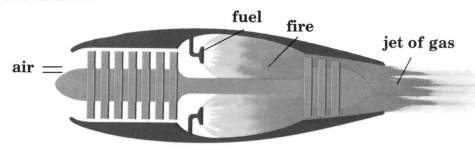

air

fuel

fire

jet of gas

A jet engine in an aircraft pulls in air and mixes it with the fuel it carries. The fuel burns and the jet of hot gases shoots out the rear of the engine to push the aircraft forward.

Spacecraft carry their own oxygen. If they did not, they could not burn their fuel in space, where there is no air.

SPACECRAFT ENGINE

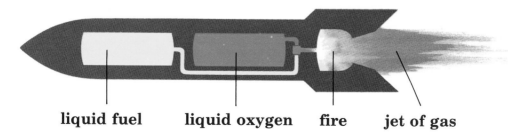

liquid fuel   liquid oxygen   fire   jet of gas

The heat from fire is used to make electricity. Electricity is made in factories called power plants. In a power plant, fuel is burned under a boiler full of water. The heat from the burning fuel boils the water and turns it to steam. The steam is used to spin a turbine rotor.

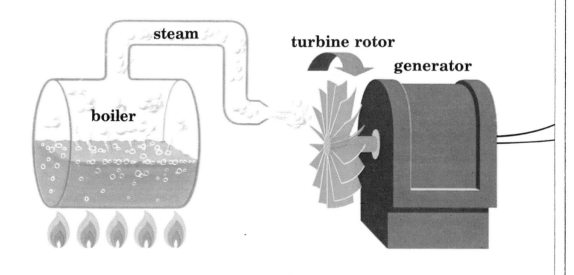

The spinning turbine rotor drives a machine called a generator. The generator makes electricity. The electricity is then sent to our homes through cables. We use electricity to make heat and light and to run machines.

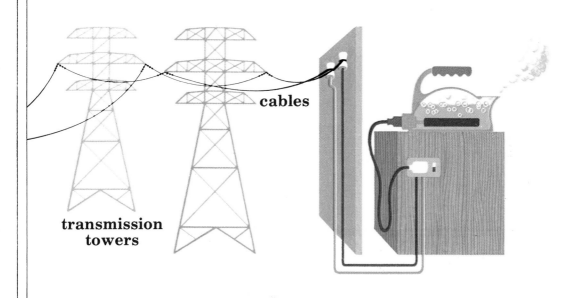

cables

transmission
towers

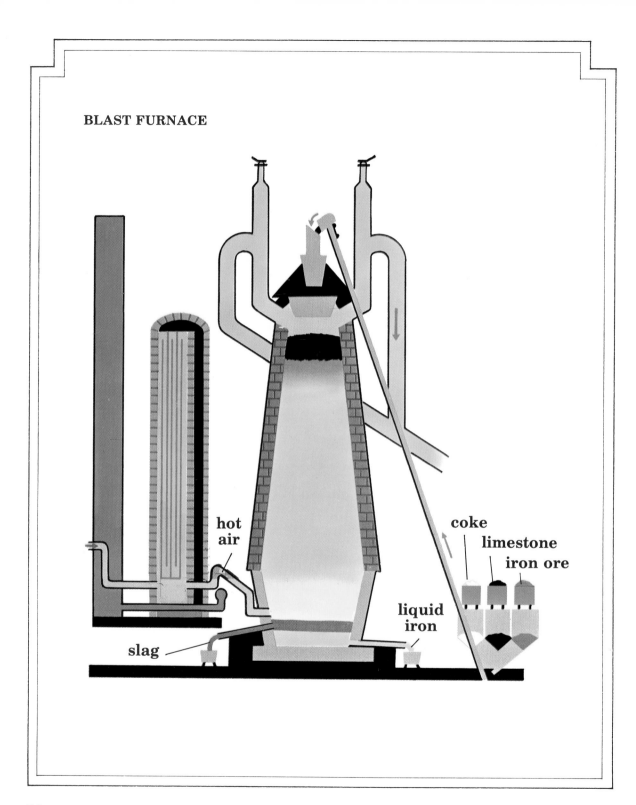

BLAST FURNACE

hot
air

coke
limestone
iron ore

liquid
iron

slag

Very hot fires can melt metals. Most metals are locked with oxygen in rocks called ores. Ores are treated in a furnace to get the metals out. This is called smelting. To get iron, iron ore is smelted in a blast furnace in this way:

1. Iron ore is poured into the top of the furnace, along with a special fuel called coke, and crushed limestone.

2. A blast of hot air blows on the coke and burns it.

3. The burning coke gives off a hot gas that unlocks the iron from the oxygen in the ore.

4. The iron melts and sinks to the bottom.

5. The sand and stone in the ore combine with the limestone to form a molten stuff called slag.

6. The slag also sinks, but it stays above the iron.

7. The iron and slag are tapped off separately at the bottom of the furnace.

We can use the fire from a cutting torch to cut metals. A cutting torch makes a very hot flame. It can also shoot a sharp stream of oxygen through this flame. The flame melts the metal. Then the stream of oxygen blows the melted metal away.

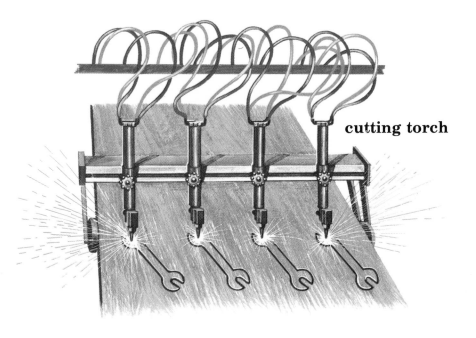

cutting torch

Gas torches are used to join, or weld, metals together. The gas flame heats the ends of the metals until they melt and fuse together. When the metals cool, they are joined together.

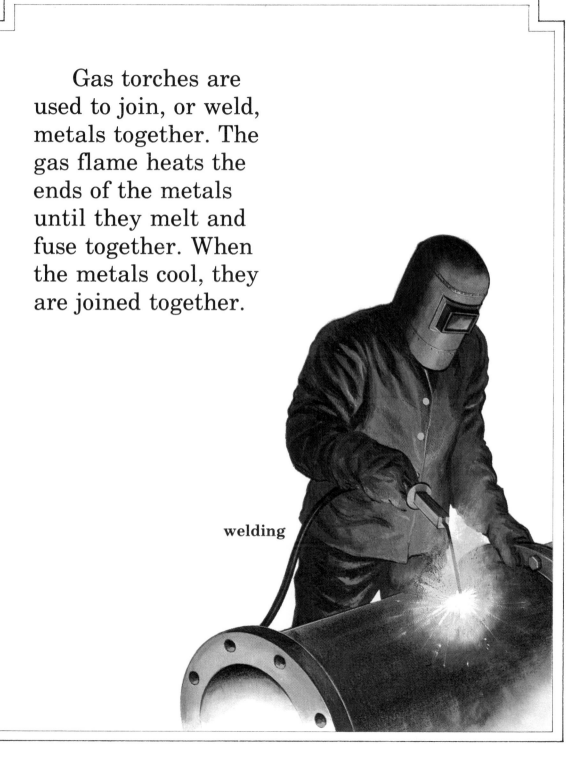

welding

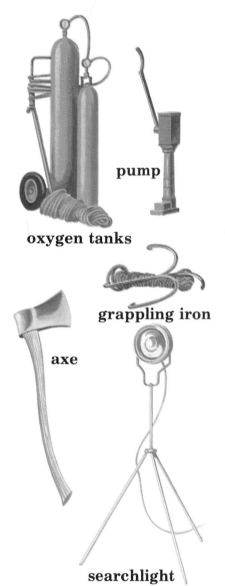

pump

oxygen tanks

grappling iron

axe

searchlight

When we can control it, fire is useful to us. When we cannot control it, fire can be very dangerous. If you see a fire, you should call the fire department. Many big buildings have fire alarms that ring in a fire station.

Fire fighters have many tools. They use axes to break open locked doors and windows. If the smoke is thick, they carry oxygen to breathe. Strong lights help them see through the smoke.

Fire fighters use water to put out most big fires. They attach long hoses to fire hydrants. Hydrants are attached to underground water pipes. A pump on the fire engine takes the water from the hydrant and forces it through the hose. The fire fighters climb tall ladders on their trucks to reach the tops of buildings.

One of the
worst fires of all is
a gas fire at an oil
well. It is so big
and fierce that it
cannot be put out
in the usual ways.

Flaming gas shoots out of the drill hole. The fire cannot be stopped by water or chemicals. The only way to put out the fire is to blast the hole shut so that no more gas can get out. People must carry explosives into the fire. They wear special clothing to protect them from the heat.

Forest fires are also hard to fight. Forest rangers are always watching for signs of a fire. They try to stop the fires from spreading. If they fail, the fires can spread for hundreds of miles. Often fires start in the middle of thick forests where there are no roads and no water. Then airplanes can be used to spray a mixture of water and chemicals from the air. Sometimes fire fighters are dropped into the forest by parachute.

Often fire fighters will make a "firebreak" to stop the fire from spreading. They cut down trees to leave an empty space in the path of the fire. The fire stops there because there is nothing more to burn.

All big fires start out as little ones. If we can put out the little fires quickly, we can prevent a lot of damage.

fire extinguisher

In most buildings we can find things that will help us put out small fires. There may be fire extinguishers. Fire extinguishers shoot out either a stream of water, foam, or gas. The water puts out a fire by cooling it. The foam or gas puts out a fire by covering it and keeping oxygen away.

Many big buildings have sprinklers to stop fires from spreading. The rooms have water pipes in the ceiling. The sprinklers are attached to the water pipes. Special metal plugs in the sprinklers melt when the room gets too hot. Water sprays out onto the fire.

sprinklers

There is fire in the sky as well as on earth. All stars are huge balls of fiery gas. They are so hot and dense that they don't need oxygen to make heat. Our sun is a star. Sometimes the moon will eclipse the sun and hide part of it from our sight. Then flames that leap hundreds of miles above the surface of the sun can be seen.

During thunderstorms, flashes of
lightning may brighten the sky. Lightning
is a powerful spark of electricity. It
heats the air as it flashes from the clouds
to the earth. Lightning is not fire, but
it can cause a fire if it hits something.

The Metric System

In the United States, things are measured in inches, pounds, quarts, and so on. That system is called the American system. Most other countries of the world use centimeters, kilograms, and liters to measure those things. That system is called the metric system.

At one time the United States was going to change to the metric system. That is why you will see both systems of measurement in some books. For example, you might see a sentence like this: "That bicycle wheel is 27 inches (69 centimeters) across."

Most books you use will have only one system of measurement. You may want to change from one system to the other. The chart on the next page will help you.

All you have to do is multiply the unit of measurement in Column 1 by the number in Column 2. Your answer will be the unit in Column 3.

Suppose you want to change 15 centimeters to inches. First, find *centimeters* in Column 1. Next, multiply 15 times .4. The answer you get is 6. So, 15 centimeters equal 6 inches.

Column 1	Column 2	Column 3
THIS UNIT OF MEASUREMENT	**TIMES THIS NUMBER**	**GIVES THIS UNIT OF MEASUREMENT**
inches	2.54	centimeters
feet	30.	centimeters
feet	.3	meters
yards	.9	meters
miles	1.6	kilometers
ounces	28.	grams
pounds	.45	kilograms
fluid ounces	.03	liters
pints	.47	liters
quarts	.95	liters
gallons	3.8	liters
centimeters	.4	inches
meters	1.1	yards
kilometers	.6	miles
grams	.035	ounces
kilograms	2.2	pounds
liters	33.8	fluid ounces
liters	2.1	pints
liters	1.06	quarts
liters	.26	gallons

Where to Read About Fire

Pronunciation Key

a	a as in **cat, bad**
ā	a as in **able, ai** as in **train, ay** as in **play**
ä	a as in **father, car, o** as in **cot**
e	e as in **bend, yet**
ē	e as in **me, ee** as in **feel, ea** as in **beat, ie** as in **piece,** y as in **heavy**
i	i as in **in, pig, e** as in **pocket**
ī	i as in **ice, time, ie** as in **tie, y** as in **my**
o	o as in **top, a** as in **watch**
ō	o as in **old, oa** as in **goat, ow** as in **slow, oe** as in **toe**
ô	o as in **cloth, au** as in **caught, aw** as in **paw, a** as in **all**
oo	oo as in **good, u** as in **put**
o͞o	oo as in **tool, ue** as in **blue**
oi	oi as in **oil, oy** as in **toy**
ou	ou as in **out, ow** as in **plow**
u	u as in **up, gun, o** as in **other**
ur	ur as in **fur, er** as in **person, ir** as in **bird,** or as in **work**
yo͞o	u as in **use, ew** as in **few**
ə	a as in **again, e** as in **broken, i** as in **pencil,** o as in **attention, u** as in **surprise**
ch	ch as in **such**
ng	ng as in **sing**
sh	sh as in **shell, wish**
th	th as in **three, bath**
<u>th</u>	th as in **that, together**

GLOSSARY

These words are defined the way they are used in this book

aircraft (er′ kraft′) a machine that
flies in the air

attach (ə tach′) to put firmly onto
something

belt (belt) a wide, flat, endless,
moving band that carries objects from
one place to another

blast (blast) a strong, swift rush
of air

boil (boil) to heat water so that it
bubbles and turns into steam

boiler (boi′ lər) a large closed-in
tank in which water is boiled

burst (burst) to break out suddenly

cable (kā′ bəl) a thick wire

cannot (kan′ ot) is not able; can not

carburetor (kär′ bə rā tər) the part of
an engine in which gasoline is mixed
with air

ceiling (sē′ ling) the top of a room

century (sen′ chər ē) one hundred years

chemical (kem′ i kəl) a substance
obtained by the science of chemistry

coal (kōl) a black substance found under the
ground and used as a fuel

coke (kōk) a grayish black substance
made from coal and used as fuel

control (kən trōl′) to have power over something

crush (krush) to squeeze something until
it breaks

cylinder (sil′ ən dər) a long, rounded,
hollow object

damage (dam′ ij) harm or injury

decompose (dē kəm pōz′) to break down
into simpler substances

dense (dens) packed thickly together

destroy (di stroi′) to ruin or wreck

drilling platform (dril′ ing plat′ fôrm)
a platform holding drilling machines
built on the water above an oil or gas site

eclipse (i klips′) when the sun or moon
is darkened or hidden

electric (i lek′ trik) having to do with electricity

electricity (i lek tris′ ə tē) a basic
property of matter; a form of energy
as an electric current

elevator (el′ ə vā′ tər) a small room or
platform that is raised or lowered to carry
things from one level to another

engine (en′ jin) a machine that uses
energy to make mechanical energy; a
machine that runs other machines

explode (eks plōd′) to burst out suddenly
from a confined space

explosion (eks plō′ zhən) the act of
hot gases suddenly bursting out of
a confined space

explosive (eks plō′ siv) something that can
cause an explosion

factory (fak′ tər ē) a building or
group of buildings where things are made

fiery (fī′ ə rē) hot and flaming

firebreak (fīr′ brāk′) an area of cleared
land intended to stop the movement of
a forest or grass fire

fire department (fīr′ di pärt′ mənt)
a place made up of a fire station,
fire fighters, and equipment

fire extinguisher (fīr′ eks ting′ gwish ər)
an instrument filled with water or
chemicals that is used to put out fires

flame (flām) the glowing gases made by a fire

flash (flash) a sudden, bright burst of light

flint (flint) a hard, gray stone used to
make sparks when hit against steel

foam (fōm) a mass of bubbles in a liquid

force (fôrs) to make something act in
a certain way by pushing or pulling

fuel (fyoo′ əl) a substance that is burned
to give heat

furnace (fur′ nis) a closed-in place where
fuel is burned

fuse (fyooz) to heat substances until they
melt and blend together

gas (gas) a substance like air in that
it is not solid or liquid

gasoline (gas′ ə lēn′) a liquid fuel used
in cars and propeller airplanes

generator (jen′ ə rā′ tər) a machine that makes electricity

glow (glō) to shine

heat (hēt) warmth; the state of being hot; to make warm or hot

hollow (hol′ ō) being empty inside like a straw

hose (hōz) a tube of some easily bent material used to carry liquids or gases from one place to another

huge (hyōōj) very big; of great size

hydrant (hī′ drənt) a strong, round, covered pipe that sticks out of the ground, to which fire fighters attach hoses for water

iron (ī′ ərn) a useful gray metal

jet (jet) a stream of hot gas

layer (lā′ ər) one thickness of a thing

lightning (līt′ ning) the powerful electrical spark that flashes from clouds to earth in thunderstorms

limestone (līm′ stōn′) a kind of rock used in blast furnaces

matches (mach′ iz) thin pieces of wood or cardboard with special chemicals on the tip to make a flame

metal (met′əl) a hard, usually shiny, substance used to make many things such as tools and machines

miner (mīn′ ər) a person who works in a mine

mix (miks) to put different things together

molten (mōlt′ ən) melted by intense heat

moon (mo͞on) the natural satellite that revolves around the earth

natural (nach′ ər əl) found in nature; not made by people

oil (oil) a greasy substance used as fuel

ore (ôr) a rock that contains a metal combined with oxygen

oxygen (ok′ sə jən) a gas necessary to life that is found in the air

parachute (par′ ə sho͞ot) a large umbrella-shaped piece of fabric attached to an object in order to slow it down as it falls

pipe (pīp) a tube used to carry gas or liquid

piston (pis′ tən) the tightly fitting
  cylinder that moves back and forth
  inside the cylindrical space in an engine

plug (plug) something used to stop up a hole

powerful (pou′ ər fəl) having a lot of
  strength or energy

prehistoric (prē′ his tôr′ ik) belonging
  to the time before people kept written
  records of events

press (pres) to push steadily against
  something

prevent (pri vent′) to stop something
  from happening

pump (pump) a machine used to force
  liquids or gases to move from one
  place to another

ranger (rān′ jər) a person whose work
  is looking after forests

raw (rô) not cooked

rough (ruf) having an uneven surface

rust (rust) a reddish brown chemical
  that forms on iron when it combines
  with oxygen

seam (sēm) a line where two materials come together

shaft (shaft) a long bar that spins around in a machine

slag (slag) a combination of limestone and the sand or rock from iron ore

smelting (smelt′ ing) to get a metal from its ore by a process that uses heat

space (spās) the area beyond the earth's atmosphere

spacecraft (spās′ kraft) a machine that travels in space

spark (spärk) a tiny bit of hot glowing material

spin (spin) to turn around and around rapidly

spray (sprā) to break a liquid into a mist of tiny drops

sprinkler (spring′ klər) a device used to shoot drops of water over a wide area

squeeze (skwēz) to press hard against something

steam (stēm) water vapor made from boiling water

steel (stēl) a metal made of iron and a small amount of carbon

strip (strip) a narrow piece of something

surface (sur′ fis) the top or outside part
of a thing

thunderstorm (thun′ dər stôrm′) a storm
that has thunder

tinder (tin′ dər) a dried substance used
to help start a fire when lit with a spark

tool (to͞ol) something that helps a person
do work

torch (tôrch) a very hot flame used to
melt metal

travel (trav′ əl) to move from one place
to another; to make a trip

tunnel (tun′ əl) an underground passage

turbine rotor (tur′ bin ro̅t′ ər) a set of
blades that spin when a stream of gas
or liquid hits them

twist (twist) to turn something
around and around

underground (un′ dər ground′) under the
ground; below the surface of the earth

weld (weld) to join metals by heating
them until they melt and fuse together

Bibliography

Broekel, Ray. *Firefighters*. Chicago:
    Childrens Press, 1981.

Bundt, Nancy. *The Fire Station Book*.
    Minneapolis: Carolrhoda Books, 1981.

Chlad, Dorothy. *When There is a Fire . . .
    Go Outside*. Chicago: Childrens Press,
    1982.

Hankin, Rebecca. *I Can be a Fire Fighter*.
    Chicago: Childrens Press, 1985.

Hannun, Dotti. *A Visit to the Fire
    Station*. Chicago: Childrens Press,
    1985.

McNulty, Sally. *Safety with Fire*.
    Windermere, Florida: Rourke, 1983.

Olesky, Walter G. *Experiments with Heat*.
    Chicago: Childrens Press, 1986.